I AM A PARAKEET

A STORY OF A PARAKEET NAMED PRINCE

YUN JI

LIBRARY TALES PUBLISHING

NEW YORK, NY

I AM A PARAKEET

Published by:

Library Tales Publishing, Inc.
1055 East Flamingo Rd #708
Las Vegas, NV, 89119
www.LibraryTalesPublishing.com

For general information on our other products and services, please contact our Customer Care Department at 1-800-754-5016, or fax 917-463-0892. For technical support, please visit www.LibraryTalesPublishing.com

Library Tales Publishing also publishes its books in a variety of electronic formats. Every content that appears in print is available in electronic books.

ISBN-13: 978-0615919560
ISBN-10: 0615919561

Dedicated to
those who love
and care for parakeets.

PREFACE

In 2011, I purchased a parakeet by chance, and today I own 10 beautiful parakeets. I am very proud and excited to present this parakeet book. During my first year as a parakeet owner, I learned how to feed them, how to tell them apart, how to understand their language and behaviors. I studied their mating rituals and the playfulness unique to this amazing species.

Parakeets make great pets. They are beautiful, funny, and expressive. They are a lot of fun to care for. This book was written for those who would like to share their love and appreciation for these amazing creatures; if you love parakeets, birds, and animals in general, you will love this book.

Please follow my page on Facebook for daily Parakeet-related posts.

Thank you.
Yun Ji
At Chicago, Illinois, USA

CONTENTS

1. BIRTH

My story begins with seven little eggs. It is Mid-October and we're getting ready to hatch.

This is My Egg!

This is our nest and that's my mom - she keeps us safe from harm.

Dad

Mommy

Mom and Dad are the best, they keep us safe inside the nest.

When I grow up, I want to be as big and strong as them!

These are my brothers and sisters. My sister HOPE is the eldest, then there are my brothers CHIP, TOM, my sister PIPPIN and... ME.

My name is PRINCE.

We rub our heads against each other, it's called preening. Everyone needs to preen! It keeps our feathers nice and clean.

It's NAP TIME!

CHIP

ME!

HOPE

TOM

5

Mom keeps us safe and warm under her wings, we all cuddle together, and it feels nice.

Parakeet babies hatch without feathers, but we develop quickly and will soon pin beautiful feathers just like Mom and Dad.

It's Lunch Time!

My family is very close. We all spend a lot of time together. We sleep, eat, and cuddle together.

As time goes by, our feathers grow and so do we. Although our nest is dark, there is still plenty of light coming from that big hole in the nest.

When Hope turned 16 days old, she grew tall enough to reach the hole, where she likes to peek outside. Sometimes I'll hear Mom sing and play around outside the nest with Dad, I can't wait until I'm old enough to be outside. At least Hope gets to peek and see what's going on.

After 14 days of rest, we saw a giant hand inside our nest. Mom says that we live with a human lady. She gives us food and water, and one day we will leave the nest and go outside to play with her. Mom also says that some parakeets can learn to talk and interact with humans, but we can't.

The human hand appeared again, and this time it brought us a new friend. She looks small and a little silly, her new name will be "Lilly."

My sister Hope is very beautiful. Her feathers are white and blue, like a pearl. Mom says that Hope will grow to look like her. Lilly is not so pretty. Her wings are black and her beak is weak.

Mom says she is a part of our family now. We all need to be nice to her and make her feel welcome.

Lilly follows me
around all the time.
I help her clean her
feathers and use her
head to preen.

After a while, we begin to get along. She's not that bad. Parakeets are very active, we like to play and are considered very intelligent.

OMG! That's Lilly's mom!

Our owner noticed that Lilly and I became good friends and one day, her hand appeared and took us both out of the nest.

If parakeets are handfed or handled when we are young, we will grow accustomed to human beings and become tame.

One day, the human moved us to a new place, a new nest. It was Lilly's old home, and I met her Mom for the first time there. Parakeets have flock-habits, and we can't be left alone or we will become depressed. If you take us away from our home, you can't expect us to be very happy.

16

Lilly was happy to see her Mom again, but I was scared, I miss my Mommy! I could still see her in the other cage, so that was a relief.

Don't be scared. My mom is nice.

Lilly's Mom became my new adoptive Mom. She fed us and took good care of us. I can sometimes see and hear my real Mom calling my name from across the room, I yell out to her through the hole, she's glad to know that I am safe. We can see each other, and the sound of her voice makes me feel safe.

Day after day, Lilly and I grew.

Our feathers became thick and fluffy and we were not so small anymore.

The human took us outside to play every once in a while. Lilly stayed by my side, as we're becoming good friends. Parakeets need daily social interactions. We like to sing and hop around, and can interact with each other, but still - it's good to interact with the human as often as possible.

Sometimes Lilly and I will be with my family in the other cage when the human cleans the cages. These were the best times because I get to spend time with my Mom. This picture was taken when I was 22 days old.

One day, I saw my sister Hope flying around the room outside the nest. She is big enough to fly! Wow! Every parakeet has his or her own unique personality, we are naturally curious and playful, and we love to spread our wings and fly around.

Mom, look at me.
I'm out!

My adoptive mom says I'm too young to fly, but I really want to try. As Parakeets, we are evolved for the purpose of flying, and there are many health benefits to it.

Lilly is 3 days younger than me, but when I turned 30 days old, my feathers became enriched and thick. Lilly grew prettier as time went by.

Mom said that a healthy parakeet will always have beautiful feathers, which is why I need to be well-fed and grow up to be a beautiful little bird.

Yes! I am finally tall enough to climb outside. I peek out and see my adoptive mom and dad, and they looked back at me, surprised.

Well, hello there.

26

Welcome!

My adopted dad
came to greet me.
They both seemed
very proud of me.
Although I missed
being with my mom
and dad, I was very
happy to be treated
so well by my
adoptive parents.

Our owner took us outside to play. She placed us inside a comfortable basket. All of these changes would have scared me when I was younger, but I am very glad and proud to have Lilly by my side. We make each other feel safe.

Help! Help!

We tried to walk around the bars, but Lilly was too scared. She could hardly hold on. She needed my help and I came to the rescue!

This is how you do it!

I showed Lilly how to hold on tight, and soon enough, we were walking around the cage together and finally had enough room to try and learn how to fly!

Today I flew for the very first time! I just spread my wings and flew away. I didn't fly far, but it was very cool. For the next few days, I could not stop staring into the big, empty space outside. So much room to fly!

Where have you been?

Flying!

I am excited to have learned this new skill. My life will never be the same.

I was growing fast and the cage suddenly didn't look so big. What once was large now appeared to be small. I could no longer fit and move around inside the nest so I had to stay outside. The cage was very big, so I could hop around freely without a worry.

Lilly and I are now the best of friends,
and our owner seems to be very happy
about it.

2. GROWING UP

Three days after I came out of the nest, Lilly finally climbed outside. It was not easy for her because she could hardly hold on to the bars, and still had trouble flying around.

I will help you.

One day, our owner moved us all to a giant cage that was almost as big as she. It had more than enough space for us to fly around. The good news is that my mom, brothers and sisters all moved in with us. We all lived happily together in that humongous cage.

In the new cage, we saw my mom and my dad again, with mom looking as beautiful as ever. My adoptive parents were also there, as well as a few others in the cage whom I had never met before. There was no screeching, biting, feather-pulling or any other signs of aggression. We got along pretty well and our owner came by often to make sure we were all getting along. Our flock is doing great! We interact, chirp, and sing together.

I didn't see Chip (my oldest brother) in the cage. Hope said that our owner placed Chip in a small cage one day and just took him away. Word is that he has a new owner now. I just hope they treat him well there. Almost everything we do is flock-oriented. Whether it's preening, eating, napping, socializing   or signing, we do it all as a flock. So, when one of our own is taken away, we feel it.

Lilly had been out of the nest for a week, but she was still pestering her mom for food. She is very headstrong and still, very spoiled.

Lilly and I chased each other around every day. We chatted, played, sang and danced; we were getting along really well. I taught Lilly how to be independent and how to eat from the container the human built for us. She no longer needs her mommy to feed her.

One thing I love about being big and strong is that I can finally use the bathtub. The humans built a large pool of water for us to bathe in and we all used it all the time.

Our adoptive parents flapped their wings and prayed water everywhere. Everyone looked pretty and clean after a bath. All parakeets have their own preferences when it comes to bathing. Some of us don't bathe at all, and others like to bathe often. Lilly and I take a bath about once every week or two, it's a lot of fun!

After a bath we would all take a nap. We nap as a flock at the same time. Whenever you see a parakeet nap, you'll notice that everyone else is napping as well.

Our naps may last about 20 to 55 minutes. Some of us nap standing on two feet, others on one foot, some of us nap with our heads forward, others with their head tucked back. We all have our favorite way of napping.

We all love to chew and gnaw on things around the cage, it's how we keep our beaks nice and strong. Our human always has a toy in the cage that is meant to be chewed on.

Hey, I am looking at you. Come up and play!

My oldest sister Hope liked to do somersaults around the perch. She wasn't very good at it, but she was having fun and we all liked watching. That is her favorite form of exercise. We need to get our exercise every day, especially in the morning after just waking up. It's a part of a healthy morning routine.

One day I was standing on the highest perch in the cage and looked outside. There were strange animals called squirrels and humans with dogs walking outside. Sometimes I would see big black birds flying in the distant sky. Mom told me that birds outside have to find their own food and many don't survive. We are very lucky to have our own human who takes care of us and feeds us.

My owner liked me the most. She always peeked into the cage and smiled at me whenever I sang. I love to sing. Most male parakeets are great singers. It is a form of entertainment for us and a great way to play and interact with our flock. It is also a great way to "show off" when we're old enough to mate and court.

One of my favorite things to do was to sit with Lilly on the perch, where we'd play and sing all day long.

As time went by, I found myself liking Lilly more and more; we were becoming the best of friends.

Sometimes we played a game called "Wild Swing." We'll hang on to the swing by our beaks and swing our bodies around the swing over and over until we got too dizzy.

One day, while everyone was playing outside, I saw Lilly standing by herself on the perch. I helped cheer her up when she was sad.

Much like humans, parakeets mate for life. Once we fall in-love with someone, we will stay together forever, mate and raise our own children happily ever after!

The next day was a
day I'll never forget.
Our owner reached
her hand into our
cage, grabbed Lilly
and placed her inside
a small, white cage.
Mom told me that I'll
be going in with her.
She said that the
humans will take us
away to mate.

The human reached
her big hand into
the cage again. Wait
a minute? No! The
human grabbed Tom,
my older brother and
placed him in the
cage with Lilly, she
locked the cage door
and took them away.
I screamed: "No!
Stop!"

I could see Lilly crying,
she was crawling
around, pinning
herself against
the bars, trying to
escape.

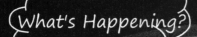

I could see them slowly drifting away in that cage as that heartless human walked away. I cried out to her, she yelled my name. She's gone, they took her away.

The humans took my Lilly away and my older brother too. Why would they do that to me? What have we ever done to them?

Then, before too long, I was alone. Sitting alone in my cage is not fun, there was no one to play with, no one to talk to and no one to love. I was alone. Most people don't get it, they think that just because we're birds we don't share the same emotions. Parakeets can get depressed too.

After a few days, my older sister Hope returned to the cage, but I still felt alone. I still felt like I was on my own, I was thinking of Lilly a lot and was hoping that one day she would come back.

That day, I stood on the top perch again, looking out. I saw a little squirrel running across the lawn, a man with a dog and a beautiful, black bird flying in the sky.

I remembered when Mom said that their freedom is "dangerous," that they have no human to feed them and take care of them. Maybe it's better that way. I started having thoughts about freedom, I wanted to be free, I want to be free with Lilly.

The next morning I woke up to the chirping sounds of a bird I did not know. I heard someone tweet and call. I looked up and ... Wow! A beautiful young bird was sitting in my basket!

How gorgeous!

The new birdie had yellow, cyan, white feathers with white spots on her back and her wings. Although her feathers were trimmed, her beauty could not be concealed. Not only was she the rare and precious species, she also was the prettiest and youngest birdie here. Her name is Daisy.

3. LOVE

I am Daisy.
I am two months old.

Daisy was young, pretty, and colorful. One of her favorite things to do was to play around the swing and gnaw the bamboo curtain.

Daisy especially liked to chew on Lilly's old bamboo baskets. She ruined every one of them, but I didn't mind. Daisy was a happy bird, always skipping and dashing everywhere with excitement. She brightened up the cage with every skip. Her excitement and energy peaked when our owner brought in a new bathtub full of water.

It's my basket!

Daisy was aggressive and very competitive. She liked to compete with Hope, my oldest sister, over the basket and the bathtub. Although she was small, Daisy had a lot of energy and charisma.

It's my place!

One day, my owner hung a new grass nest in our cage. It was very cute, we all liked it. Daisy and I ran towards it to see who would get there first. Long story short, my adoptive mom dislodged us both and took over the grass nest. Moms always go first!

Daisy and I were attracted to each other, and I couldn't keep my eyes away from her breathless beauty.

I often followed her wherever she went and always tried to be around, trying to win her attention by showing off my beautiful white feathers, signing and bobbing my head to show off.

I was three months old around the time that I began to woo Daisy. She did not make it easy for me. One day, I was trying to get closer, but got too close and she unceremoniously bit me and made me fall down the perch.

Outch!

I respected Daisy's space and kept away for a little while, but as time went by Daisy and I became closer. We began to bond.

Daisy and I had a deal. If I saw the human place a long piece of delicious millet sprays, I would call her immediately and we would get there before the other birds found out. I became her protector, whenever she ate I would be at her side, guarding her like a royal soldier.

Daisy and I loved washing and trimming our feathers. I thought she looked really beautiful and she said that she loves the sound of my voice.

When my adoptive mom finally left the grass nest, I called Daisy to follow me in. While Daisy played inside of the nest, I stood watch outside, just in case mom came back. I finally got Daisy's recognition.

Prince, you are so charming.

Daisy began to accept me. We were courting each other and getting ready to mate. I sang and bobbed my head at her, as well as fed her regurgitated food. We began to touch beaks, as well as preen each other's head and cheek feathers. We stuck together!

Daisy and I were now boyfriend and girlfriend. We were with each other all the time.

On one sunny morning, I proposed to Daisy and asked if she would be my wife. Daisy accepted and we officially became a couple. I swore I would love and protect her and whenever I saw any male birds coming around, I'd rush them away without hesitation.

One day, I was playing on the top of the cage when I saw that my owner placed a new cage on the other side of the room, she took our favorite swing and Daisy's favorite basket and placed them inside.

The owner let us walk inside it, this was our new home.

said goodbye to my mom and my dad, their son had grown up.

I said goodbye to my oldest sister. She still did her somersaults around a perch and had yet to improve.

I said goodbye to my adoptive mom and my dad. I would not forget how well they treated me.

Daisy and I moved in the new place and started our new life together. We were about four months old at the time.

Keep reading, our story is just beginning.

4. BREEDING

Daisy and I moved into our new home. It was cozy and comfortable and we had everything we needed. No one bothered us. No one disturbed us. We had the freedom to do as we pleased, and it was time for us to start our lives together.

We kissed all the time and spent every waking moment together. I felt my life was so sweet and so wonderful.

We checked our nest and planned carefully. Our babies would be born there and grow up here, this will be our home for a while.

Yeah, it looks comfortable.

Do you like the nest?

Daisy went in and out of the nest frequently, adapting to the environment and getting herself familiar with the nest. I often stood on the station bar of the nest, looking at Daisy and asking her if there was anything I could do.

Everything was ready and it was finally time to mate. We were young and new at mating, but we complemented each other well and made sure that everything was perfect. Breeding season starts in October and ends in March. Parakeets need to have a comfortable environment and to be healthy and happy to breed.

Daisy began gnawing on cuttlefish bones because she knew that she was going to lay eggs soon and needed to get enough calcium to ensure the health of our babies.

After one week of mating, Daisy laid the first egg. Several days past before she laid another, and another, until reaching a total of five eggs. It was not easy for Daisy. Laying eggs was hard work, but she did a great job!

Parakeet eggs take about 18-22 days to hatch, and the most comfortable temperatures to keep the eggs is 65 to 75 degrees. We are both very excited and also very patient!

Most of the time, Daisy stayed inside the nest, hatching eggs. She only came out when she needed to drink water or take a short break. She was working very hard and soon became tired and weak.

I did my best to feed her. I ate a lot and fed her many times each day, that's a man's job!

It was my job to keep watching after her and to give her enough energy so that she has the strength to hatch our babies. Daisy has a lot of freedom. The Human rarely opens the cage and when she does, she only interacts with me.

With the exception of Feeding Daisy, I still had plenty of time on my hand, and since Daisy always stayed in the nest, I felt bored. Often, I would stand on the top of the cage and play by myself while still keeping an eye on Daisy. I'd also stare at my owner to see what she was doing.

My owner noticed how bored I was and placed a new toy swing for me. I liked the small bell beneath the swing that made a cool sound every time I pecked it. The day of hatching was coming. I felt excited and nervous.

Finally, after Daisy's 18 days in the nest, our first baby came out of the shell. It was a boy! He was so tiny. The babies will hatch every other day in the order they were laid. Every other day, another egg would hatch and our two daughters came into the world! Daisy and I were so happy to take care of them and to feed them.

We knew before too long, our babies would grow their feathers and fly. They will get to wander around the cage, get into trouble, meet new friends, play, look outside, wonder, get their heart broken, and fall in love all over again. That's life and we're happy to give it to them.

[THE END]

Want to keep up with Prince
and Daisy?

Visit www.IAmAParakeet.com
Or follow us on Facebook.

53333947R00066

Made in the USA
Middletown, DE
26 November 2017